Confessions of A Baptist Minister

"The Best is Yet to Be"

Jimmy C. Bryant

Dedicated to my wife of fifty-eight years, who has encouraged me to author a book for years.

The best helpmate that God could ever give a preacher.

One of the most thoughtful and wisest persons I have known.

Grow old along with me!

The best is yet to be.

The last of life, for which the first was made.

Our times are in His hand who saith

"A whole I planned, Youth shows but half;

Trust God: See All, nor be afraid".

- Robert Browning

Contents

CHAPTER ONE

Gone Fishin'

John Roberts was born into a sharecroppers' family. I do not know what you know about share croppers, but they do not have much and never will have much. The home into which John was born lived his great-grandmother, grandmother, grandfather, and mother. Early in John's life, his grandfather gave up on the sharecropper's life and moved to another town where he went to work for Kraft Foods in a cheese plant. It brought a steady income and he was able to buy a three-bedroom house. A few years later, he was able to add another bedroom and a bathroom to the back of the house. Not having to go to the outhouse to use the bathroom was the grandest day of John's life. He grew up playing under the house, on a mimosa tree in the front yard, a chinaberry tree in the backyard, and a sagebrush patch to the side of the house. He also wandered back and forth between home and a little store run by a kindly man, Joe who did not mind John spending time together there, where the old men of the community also spent time together, playing checkers, and telling tall tales.

Occasionally, John would crave a candy bar and soft drink so badly that he would get them and put it on his mother's bill. When she would come every week to settle with Joe, she would always owe more than she thought. Looking over the receipts, she would finally get to the ones where John had charged something. She would scold him, but it did little good when his cravings got the best of him. As a kid of nine- or ten-years-old John learned more sitting outside, somewhere around the checkers' table, than he ever learned in school.

He thoroughly enjoyed hearing the old men's stories and he relived them in his mind over and over again.

In the 1940s, Northeast Mississippi offered a variety of real characters. Farmers, factory workers, clerical workers, and even unemployed folks. Women who cooked three meals a day from scratch and worked alongside their husbands in the fields or in factories and kept the house as neat as a pin while making it look easy. Men who were hunters, fishermen, sawmillers, factory workers, those who never worked, and many odd ones with no desire to do such trivial things as hunt or fish. Some were fun-loving family men who came from humble backgrounds and were stuck there, while others were sourpusses born with a silver spoon in their mouth and wanted you to know it.

The men talked so much about fishing that John developed a real hankering to go fishing. The closest body of water where John could "fish" was a wet-weather creek down below his house. On those days when he bugged her long enough, his grandmother would find a long stick, tie some sewing thread to one end of the stick and a bobby pin on the other end. John would find a worm or two and off he would go to that little wet-weather creek that ran under the road just below his house. About all he ever caught was a turtle or two and a few crawfish. However, in his mind, he was living the life that he heard the old men talk about. They talked about fishing, and he was fishing! He had no shame when he bragged about it to the checkers' players.

The characters who shaped John Roberts' life were men and women like Tom Smith, who was a Jake-leg carpenter, (which is kind of like a shade tree mechanic) who was glad for an inquisitive little boy to follow him around. Tom also had a cotton field just across the gravel road from where John lived, and he always let him hold the reins of his mules while he adjusted the straps and harnesses. He never seemed to tire of giving answers to the prying little boy. Then, there was Mr. Clarence who let Johnny ride with him in the big truck, delivering lumber from the sawmill to his customers. He was not much bigger than a straw, but he was married to a woman who made up for it. (If she had been two inches taller, she would have been round.) They had no children but seemed to love John and loved having him around. And best of all, there was Mrs. Agnes Stovall who invited him to eat a formal lunch with her occasionally. She was old, very elegant, and seemed to enjoy having a little boy eat with her from time to time. She set the table with cloth napkins and real silverware. Over time, she taught that little tow-headed kid the proper use of each item on the table, from knives to napkins.

People like these along, with three incredibly special women - his great grandmother, grandmother, and mother - helped to shape John into what he became. John was never sure whether his great grandmother had feet and legs or not. He never saw them. She just floated across the floor with her hair put up in a bun and her homemade flour sack dress dragging on the floor. John's mother worked in a shirt factory and was not home except after work and on weekends. You would think a privileged child like him would be spoiled rotten. Not a chance. Of course, all those people and the homes in which they lived are gone today, but the memories live on in John's mind. He found that after fifty-five years, he can remember things from the 1940s better than he can remember his great grandchildren's names.

John was the product of a broken home. His father left him and his mother when John was only an infant. As unusual as it is, his mother never spoke ill of his father, at least in his presence. But people in his small Mississippi town loved John's father and he would swell with pride when someone would say, "aren't you Clyde Roberts' boy?" John was an only child until his mother remarried a man who did not have much use for him, and John had little use for him. When his stepfather was at work or out drinking, John was happiest. because it was just him and those three female institutions in his life. John was so unhappy when his stepfather was at home that he could not wait to get away. Even the two weeks in summer that he spent with his father, whom he really did not know, it was a pleasure just being away from home.

Most of John's life was spent around older people and he enjoyed every minute of it. However, he did have one playmate who lived close by, Jerry Wooley. Jerry's dad ran a little hole-in-the-wall café in the middle of town. He was as straight as an arrow in his faith. However, a rumor circulated through town that when a carnival came to town, he almost lost everything at a gambling booth. I am not sure he ever got over the embarrassment of that little episode. Every Saturday Jerry's folks would invite John to go to church with them the next day. Most of the time he took them up on their invitation. First Baptist Church had a good youth program and John enjoyed all the activities, especially ping-pong. As it turns out, that youth program was important to John's spiritual development.

One summer Sunday night when the pastor finished his sermon and gave the invitation, Jerry went forward. This alter call was asking people who wanted to make a new commitment to Christ to come forward. John really did not understand why Jerry did this, but a couple of verses of the invitation hymn later something got hold of John's heart and he came under deep conviction. A moment later he found himself walking the longest aisle he had seen before or since. Like a child without a lot of understanding, he went forward and gave his heart to Jesus as best as he knew how. He went home that night and told his mother and she seemed disappointed. Perhaps it was because she was not a regular in the church at the time. She thought he was too young and could not understand about trusting Christ. That was the beginning and the end of the discussion. John did not remember it being mentioned again until he was baptized.

John kept going to church with Jerry for several years but eventually began to drift away. He found some new friends who were not Christian, and they all did some very unchristian things. He began to smoke and drink. The cigarettes made him almost cough up a lung and the beer made him almost vomit, but he kept it up, so he could be like these cool, rowdy friends he fell in with.

As John grew up, he became more rambunctious. He hated school and was known to be a problem student. He became quite familiar with the principal's office. In the ninth grade, he dropped out of school and began to hang around a truck stop on the outskirts of town.

During this time, John had two or three jobs. He worked at a drive-in café for a while and got to the point where he actually ran the café from midnight until morning. Then, an older friend got him a job as a fill-in projectionist at a drive-in theatre.

CHAPTER TWO

Navy Days

On the day John turned seventeen, he joined the United States Navy. They took him to Birmingham, Alabama, kept him overnight, gave him a physical, swore him in, gave him a train ticket and orders to report to Great Lakes Naval Training Center in Great Lakes, Illinois. All of this to a boy who had hardly been out of Pocono county in Mississippi. Following boot camp at Great Lakes, God surely directed the hands of those who prepared the orders, as they sent John to report to the Naval Training Center at Bainbridge, Maryland for Radio Operator's School. Uneducated kids like John just did not get that kind of opportunity in the military. At school, he learned typing, Morse code, semaphore, and how to maintain and repair electronic equipment.

Following several months of Radio School, his first duty assignment was aboard the USS General George M. Randall. This was also an assignment that most Navy radiomen only lust after. Luckily, it was John's duty station and it was the easiest time that he spent in the Navy. Later, John would be transferred to the USS Chilton. The Randall was a gigantic taxi that shuttled Military Dependents from New York to places like Bremerhaven, Germany, South Hampton, England. Thessalonica, Greece, and other Mediterranean ports. This was the ship that transported Elvis Presley to his duty station in Germany. John met Elvis and thought he was the nicest young man you could ever meet. One night, there was a talent show aboard ship. Usually, only a few men attended, but this night the mess hall was overflowing in anticipation of Elvis singing. Unfortunately, he did not take part because of contractual considerations. That night, the mess hall was filled with disappointed sailors.

The Chaplain was the Educational Officer aboard the Randall. He talked to John about getting his GED and he finally did get a degree from the United States Armed Forces Institute, but it was only to pass the time on the Atlantic crossing. The Navy actually gave John more education in four years than many people get in a lifetime of formal schooling. Interestingly, the Chaplain never once mentioned the Lord to John. Strange how sometimes the tremendously important things never get talked about.

Toward the end of John's enlistment, he transferred to the Submarine School in New London, Connecticut. The Navy gave him fifteen days leave before the school was to begin. He went home during that time and a friend, Bobby introduced him to the prettiest, shiest girl he had ever met. Often, love, at first sight, can be cured by a second look, but that was not the case with John. He decided right then that he was going to marry that girl, and sure enough, they were married in 1960. He was going on twenty-one and Annie had just turned seventeen. Annie was a high school senior and they were both as green behind the ears as a spring sapling.

Annie was also the product of a broken home. Her father was a rough commercial fisherman, who left the family when Annie was a little girl. Her older brother, Roy went to live with his dad and Annie stayed with her mother. Like John, they never had much of this world's goods. And, like John, she had a challenging time with a stepparent. When Annie was fifteen, she went to live with her father and stepmother. Life there was pure torment.

In order to take the training at New London's Submarine School, John had agreed to extend his enlistment two more years. After meeting Annie, he decided that he did not want to spend those added years in the Navy, so he declined to extend his enlistment. In short order, they shipped him out to Norfolk, Virginia and assigned him to the USS Chilton, a troop transport, which was just another taxi taking soldiers to their duty stations.

Not long after John and Annie were married, he moved Annie to Norfolk into a little two-room apartment on Little Creek Road. John had rented the apartment and got it ready for his new bride.

It was all stocked up with groceries and two bottles of Jack Daniels. John had progressed from a few beers to the hard stuff. He went back to Mississippi and brought Annie to their new home. She was like a kid opening a birthday present, as she looked through all the cabinets and opening every drawer and door. When she came to the cabinet where the Jack Daniels was, she looked John straight in the eye and said, "I will not have this in my house, pour it out right now". John did so and never drank again.

His ship was scheduled to go into dry dock for repairs and he was not supposed to go back to sea before his discharge date. But one morning as John returned to the ship, he noticed that they were taking down all the lines and cables. When he went aboard, he was told not to call or write to anyone because they were about to embark with a shipload of soldiers to some undisclosed location. As it turned out, some dictator was killed in one of the South American countries and John spent two weeks cruising back and forth along the country's ocean boundaries.

In the meantime, Annie was living in their new home wondering if this man she married only a few weeks earlier had deserted her or if something awful had happened to him and no one knew how to contact her. But one of the other Navy wives in the apartment complex told her what had probably happened. That was little comfort to a new bride in a strange place where she knew absolutely no one. She stayed in that apartment not having a soul to talk to except herself. And, she did that just to make sure she could still talk. But sure enough, in about two-weeks, John showed up again to find her almost sick with worry. She only had a few cans of vegetables left to eat and no way to go anywhere to buy anything. Thankfully, the rest of John's enlistment was spent in port.

CHAPTER THREE

Vacuum Cleaners

After John's discharge, they moved to Memphis, Tennessee and lived in the house with John's father and stepmother. Not the most ideal situation, but it beat living on the streets. At that time, jobs - real family supporting jobs - were hard to come by. However, it was not many days until John got his dream job. He was hired and trained to sell shell homes. After a couple of days of training, John knew he could never make it in that field. So, he went back to job hunting.

Right off the bat, he landed another job, this time selling vacuum cleaners. He was assigned a salesperson to travel around with him to learn the tricks of the trade. Late one evening, John made a sale of an expensive vacuum cleaner to an elderly lady who appeared not to be able to afford it; she did not even have a rug in the house much less carpet. John knew he could not continue to do that because his heart would not let him take advantage of anyone.

Memphis has given him two potential careers that he gave up before he even got started. He, Annie, and his dad talked it over and they decided to move to Tupelo, Mississippi where he and Annie went to work in a coat factory. They were living from payday to payday but having an enjoyable time as newlyweds. John and Annie had been married about a year when she came home from a routine doctor visit and broke the delightful news that she was pregnant. In 1962, the Lord gave them their first child, a son, whom they named Mark. They were like two kids, playing with that baby like it was a doll.

Like many young couples, John and Annie did not attend church. They usually visited family on the weekends. However, not long after the birth of their son, a little lady from a church near where they lived came by and told them she heard they had a new baby and would be tickled to death to have them bring him to church and enroll him in the "Cradle Roll." They decided to show off the most handsome baby that ever lived, so they took her up on her invitation. They began to attend church and really enjoyed it; they especially loved the pastor, who was a kind, loving man.

One Sunday morning, Annie began to weep as the pastor began his message. Just light sniffing at first, but as his sermon progressed so did her weeping. Now it was not sniffing, it was full-blown sobbing. John was embarrassed and wondered if folks sitting around them would think he beat her the night before. When the pastor gave the invitation to come forward to the altar, Annie shot out past John. About that time, John had come under deep conviction and he also went forward. They both made a real recommitment of their lives to the Lord. Both were saved when they were young, but never really grew or matured in their relationship with the Lord.

Annie's mother was not a church-going woman, but she did hire a taxi to come to pick Annie up and take her to church every Sunday. The organist always insisted that Annie sit in the front pew with her when the music was finished. Annie always thought she had her sit there to keep her eye on that little girl that had no family in the church. Annie accepted Christ as her Savior while attending that church. Being saved young would cause some concern for Annie and John as they grew older.

It is easy to see how this rededication experience was almost as meaningful to them as the day each of them was saved. This was their first of several decisions concerning Christ as adults. They became active in all the programs of the church and saw to it that everyone met their gorgeous baby boy. As people made over the baby, John would swell with pride. After all, he looks just like me John would think to himself.

John and Annie, like many young couples, were working and still living from payday to payday. On one occasion, the coat factory was shut down for a week. This meant that John and Annie would not get a paycheck that week. There was too much week left at the end of the money and they realized that they did not have enough money to buy the baby his formula. John went to a little community grocery store where they sometimes bought things. He asked the owner if he would hold a ten-dollar check until the next week when they would get paid. Without giving it a moment's thought, he said, "no." John left there as mad as a wet hen and went to the pharmacy where they filled their prescriptions and asked the owner the same thing. Again, without a moment's hesitation he said, "sure, I think we can do that." John got the ten dollars, bought the formula, and had a little money in his pocket. That day or the next, John and Annie received a refund check from an encyclopedia company because they had overpaid for a set of encyclopedias while living in Virginia. It was in the amount of twelve dollars and some few cents. You could never make John and Annie believe anything except that it was the Lord taking care of His children. It would be hard to explain how much this increased their faith in the scriptural truth that God would take care of them if they lived for Him.

CHAPTER FOUR

The Call

Several months passed and the Lord began to stir John's heart about preaching. That was one of the most unexpected things God had done in his life, before or since. John struggled with trying to understand all God was speaking to his heart about. He felt the call to preach but felt God had the wrong address. John felt that the way he had lived while in the Navy, and before, would disqualify him from such a calling. After all, John had several tattoos on his arms. But the Lord was relentless and finally convinced John that it was His will for him to preach.

John knew that he would have to further his education to do an acceptable job, so he and Annie gave their notices at work and began to pack up what little they had and move from Tupelo to Booneville, so John could begin his formal education at Northeast Mississippi Junior College. If the Chaplain on John's ship had not convinced him to get his GED, he would not have been able to enroll in college. So, God was at work in John's life back then and John was not even aware of it. John and Annie both got jobs by the time they were moved into their new apartment. When registration began at the Community Junior College, John went to register for English 101. He certainly needed this course because his English was awful, and he did not know a noun from a verb. He told the department head his background and lack of formal education and that the Lord had called him to preach and he wanted to prepare himself. Then, he asked the sixty-four-thousand-dollar question. "do you think I have a chance in English 101?" Without blinking an eye, the department head Mrs. Krueger, who was doing the registering said, "not a chance", and refused to register him. Boy did his feathers fall, but he left that room, went down the hall, and successfully registered in Psychology 101.

John worked days and went to school at night and worked nights and went to school on days. He felt like he could do brain surgery when he graduated from Northeast Mississippi Junior College with an Associate of Arts degree. He continued his education even as he pastored and graduated from Blue Mountain College in Blue Mountain, Mississippi with a double major in Bible and Social Studies and earned a Bachelor of Arts degree. John used to laugh and tell folks that he was proud to be a Blue Mountain Girl. You see, Blue Mountain College was a Mississippi Baptist College for girls and only recently allowed men who had been called to the Christian ministry to attend there. John eventually went on to Florence State University in Florence, Alabama to do master's work in psychology. The university is now known as the University of North Alabama at Florence. What would that lady registering English 101 think about his chances now?

John talked to his pastor and to the Associational Missionary, asking them to help him find opportunities to preach. But there was so many retired preachers and preachers without churches who were already known to the congregations that it was almost impossible for John to get an opportunity to preach. John finally received an invitation to preach at a little country church. The pastor was going to Saint Louis to see the Cardinal's play ball. When John finished his sermon and extended an invitation for people to respond, one woman came forward accepting Christ as her personal Savior. It was the grandest day John had to that point. He eventually received more opportunities to preach and the Lord truly blessed his ministry.

CHAPTER FIVE

The Preacher & The Mayor

The thought of transitioning from ordinary-three-times-a-week-church-attender to the leader of the flock made both John and Annie uneasy. They were so green that they did not really know what pastors did. In addition, they did not know how to do a lot of the things that pastors do. All John knew to do was to work and wait. He studied and tried to prepare sermons, so he would be ready to preach when he had the opportunity. The waiting was awful. It seemed like the opportunity to preach would never come. John was eventually asked to preach several times a month at what was called The Old Folks Home. It was not what he had hoped for, but it would do for now. Besides, he was getting some much-needed experience.

One morning the Associational Missionary called and asked John if he could preach the following Sunday because the regular pastor had another commitment. Sunday morning finally arrived, and John, Annie, and little Mark drove the 30 miles to the church. By this time, Annie was expecting their second child. One of the first people John met was the former pastor who remained in the church as a member after his resignation. That was when John's heart fell, and his earlier excitement turned into intimidation. This pastor was blind, had to sit to preach, and had been their pastor for more than 45 years. That was a hard act to follow.

When it came time for the sermon, the chairman of deacons, an older, sweet-spirited man, introduced him. John preached his heart out, and after his sermon was finished, there was suddenly a voice that must have sounded like God's when he spoke to Moses on Mount Sinai. The voice was that of the former pastor. He said, ***"I didn't hear anyone invite this young man back next Sunday"***. With that not so subtle prodding, the chairman of deacons came over and invited John to speak the following Sunday.

John preached several Sundays and then one Sunday the deacon chairman announced that in two Sunday's they would vote on whether to call him as pastor. The church voted unanimously that he become their pastor. John and Annie were thrilled beyond measure; their dream had finally been fulfilled. Though the church was small, the people had great hearts. John instinctively knew that this was the church that every young pastor should serve first as he began his ministry.

It was not long until John realized that this little country church had the same variety of people that he grew up around in his hometown: fishermen, farmers, factory workers, and hunters. One of the men, an avid hunter, usually killed something on his hunting trips in places like Colorado and Montana. He always brought John a pheasant from his hunting trips. John would take it, thank him profusely, put it in the deep freeze, and after a respectable amount of time would throw it in the garbage. After all, Annie did not even know how to get the feathers off. And, really now, who would want to eat one of the ugly things anyway?

This was the church where John learned what it meant to be a pastor. Eating in their homes after Sunday Services, receiving their fresh kill, dressing a mess of fish, and enjoying fellowships after the evening service, he learned something about the heart of the people. They were deeply caring, generous to a fault, filled with love for their pastor family and God-honoring in their lifestyle. John and Annie became especially close to one family, and though the man is now in heaven, they stay connected with his wife, after more than fifty years.

The church family could not believe that Annie did not work with children and youth, did not teach a Sunday school class, nor play the piano. John would tell folks that Annie was so shy that folks did not know he was married the first three years he pastored the church. Even after several years of marriage, Annie was still that shy girl that John met when he came home on leave from the Navy, and she was still just as pretty. But one Sunday, her personality changed.

Her shyness had disappeared. She went to the backdoor with John to greet the people as they left services. She shook their hands, talked with them, and enjoyed every minute. The Lord worked a miracle in Annie's life in enabling this extremely shy young woman to flourish. Both John and the church were thrilled to see that she became more outgoing, a desirable quality for a preacher's wife. Although she is still quiet and shy most of the time, Annie is a woman of great wisdom. Had John listened to her advice through the years, some of the trouble he found himself in could have been avoided.

In the early months of John's new pastorate, Annie gave birth to their second son, Luke. He, too, was the most handsome little boy you have ever seen. Now, it was like they had two dolls to play with, although there were times when both were crying, wanting to be fed or changed. Reality set in and they realized that these wonderful gifts from the Lord are not dolls. The church family was so supportive and so affectionate to the pastor's children. At Christmas time, almost every member of the church family would have a gift under the tree for Mark and Luke. By the way they acted, it seemed like each one of them was the children's grandparent. It was a wonderful time of growing and adjusting to the vocation that John and Annie had devoted their lives to. They also devoted and dedicated those two sons to the Lord. The Lord gave them to them, and they felt led to give them back to the Lord, as best as was humanly possible.

The church was about thirty miles from the Robert's home. They had a little Volkswagen Beetle, that had two-forty air conditioning. That is where you roll two windows down and drive forty miles an hour to get cool. On many Sunday afternoons, rather than drive the thirty miles back home, Annie made the two boys a pallet by letting the back seat down and they would sleep while waiting for the evening service.

It was in this church that John conducted his first baptism. Several had received Christ as Savior, ranging in age from teenagers to one of the older deacons' wife. The church had no baptistry. Where the baptistry would normally be in a church there was a fan that was as big, and as loud, as an airplane propeller at full tilt. John had to learn to raise his voice so they could hear him. Anyway, instead of a baptistry, they used a pond that was located near the church, in one of the members' pasture. That Sunday afternoon the church family gathered around one side of the pond for the first baptizing the church had had in quite a long time. John was filled with fear and trembling, as well as joy and excitement.

Two things John was deathly afraid of: water and snakes. Going into a pond where he could not see the bottom was horrifying to him. Those gathered for this long-awaited event first sang a song and John called on one of the men to pray. Then, like Joshua as he led the Hebrews to the Promised Land, John stepped off into the water. When he did, he thought his legs went numb (do not know if it was fear or the freezing water), and he thought he would freeze to death. The pond was fed by a cold-water spring and overgrown with vegetation around most of the edge. John could see himself and the converts being overcome with moccasin bites. Had something touched him on the leg, he would have drowned whoever he had in the water at the time or walked on water getting out of there. Those gathered for the big event thought it was funny, but John thought, "we need to build a baptistry".

John learned something from each of the churches he pastored. However, it was here that he learned the basics of being a pastor, such as just dropping by for a minute meant the world to people, whether you caught them at the house or at the barn, or in the field. He learned that these people were honored to share a meal with them. The greatest lesson was that preaching prowess was not as important as your ability to genuinely care for the people.

John also learned that it did not take much to ruffle some feathers. For several decades, the church had not received an offering during the worship service and as a result, it hurt for money. The former pastor had faithfully served the church for 47 years and he did not believe that unchurched people should give to the church. So, if you wanted to donate money, you either gave through your Sunday School class or you handed it to one of the deacons. Well, John felt it was a vital part of the worship service to give the opportunity for contributions to be made to the ministry. He had a business meeting with the deacons, and they voted to start passing the offering plates during the worship service. Since the former pastor opposed it and when the proposal passed, he decided that he would move his membership to a church closer to his home. And, by the way, they also passed the offering plates in their church as well. John tried to present his view to this wise, but strong-willed former pastor, but John was not successful in changing his mind.

Another thing that bothered John was the budget. There were only three items in the budget: the pastor received fifty percent of the offerings, twenty-five percent was given to missions, and the other twenty-five percent went for the upkeep. This was fine when John first went there, but as the church grew, so did the offerings and John felt it was not fair to give the pastor fifty percent of the offerings. However, as persuasive as he tried to be in helping them set a unified budget, he was never able to convince the church to do it any other way.

One of the men in the church was a mentally challenged man, George, who was probably in his fifties and was deeply loved by every member. At some point in years past they had given him the job of standing up front holding "The Birthday Jar," which was a quart fruit jar that his mother had wrapped a piece of cloth around for decoration, and people with a birthday that week would come forward and put a penny for every year of their life in this birthday jar. He always sat on the first row with his father and another elderly man, Mr. Cross an old timber broker. It seems at the close of every service, as an invitation to decide for Christ was given, George would turn and look at the congregation with tears welling up in his eyes. John always thought he did that, hoping and perhaps praying, that someone would come forward. He was not a distraction, he was an encouragement.

When John left that church, he missed George and his tender heart more than anyone or anything. At the time, he did not realize what an inspiration he was. It was years later that John finally began to understand all that he learned from those people and that church. It was there that he discovered as a young preacher that the best is yet to be.

During their years at John's first church, they were bi-vocational. John was an on-air personality at WVOM radio in a small town in Mississippi. He opened the broadcast day Monday through Saturday at 5:00 a.m. and was there until noon and after. It was his first job in radio. He did the announcing, cut the commercials, and played the music. Almost like a one-man band. It worked out well, as Annie was working in a factory during the day and John went to college in the afternoon or evenings to try and gain all the much-needed education he could. They just sort of grunted at each other as they passed, like two ships in the night.

Not many months passed until he was offered a similar job in a larger station, WBIP in his hometown in Northeast Mississippi. It was closer to home and paid a little more, so he jumped on it. The hours were about the same, except he did not have to work past noon and no Saturdays. He fit in well with the other employees and one of them, "Big Mel" Felton, gave him an "on air" nickname as, "The Morning Mayor!" The nickname stuck and he was able, through comments he could make from time to time, to say a word for Christ and point men to Him.

However, these were tough years. John and Annie had two little boys, they were buying their first home, they only had one car, and their work schedules did not come close to being convenient. He had to go on the air at 5:00 a.m., so Annie would get up around 4:00 a.m., they would gather Luke and Mark and lay them in the backseat of the car. She would take him to the station, return home, put the boys back in their beds, clean house, fix breakfast, get the boys up, get them fed, deliver them to the baby sitter, come back to the station with John's breakfast, and still get to work before 7:00 a.m. She would pick him up on her lunch hour, he would take her back to work and go to class at the college. John would be finished about the time she got off, he would pick her up, they would get the boys, go home, and get ready to do it all over again the next day. Between her job and his, school, two sons and the church, which was about thirty miles from home, they had little, if any time left. However, in looking back over the years, those days became the fulfillment of the best is yet to be.

CHAPTER SIX

Ole Porkchop

After being at his first church for about four years, pastor search committees began to contact John to see if he would be interested in making a move. One day, he was contacted by one of the most notable and respected country churches in the Association. He met with them and preached a trial sermon on Sunday morning and Sunday night services. Following the evening service, the chairman of deacons asked John, Annie, and the boys to step outside the building while they had a discussion. After just a minute or two, one of the men came to the door and asked them to come back. They had voted on whether to call John to be their pastor and the vote was unanimous. They were shocked that the church voted so soon; they figured it would take a week or more. John and Annie had already been praying about it and felt led to accept their call.

Ending the relationship with John's first church was one of the most difficult tasks of his life so far. He had no idea that every time he would move, it would be the same way. He felt God calling him to this new church, so the following Sunday he gave his current church a thirty-day notice. He and Annie cried all the way home following his resignation.

Now that the Roberts' was moving to a larger, "full-time" church, John and Annie had to give up their jobs, their friends, and their home, move away and leave the only church he had any experience with as a pastor. It meant that "The Morning Mayor" would have to relinquish his title and give up the only job he ever had that he genuinely loved, as much as preaching. It also meant that John and Annie would be dependent on the church for their livelihood. No overtime income, no way of knowing if these people would love and care for him and his family the way their former church had. But they were convinced that the Lord had opened this as a door of opportunity, therefore, He would provide for them.

By the time they were ready to move, they had rented their home. However, the rent barely paid the mortgage payment. John was constantly having to call a plumber or electrician to fix some little glitch that he could have taken care of if he had lived closer. It got to the point that some months they spent more on minor repairs than they received in rent. They decided the best thing they could do was offer to let the renter buy the house just by taking over the mortgage and making the payments. It may have been a foolish decision, but that seemed to be the only way they would ever have any peace, emotionally or financially.

Since John did not have a secular job and he was new to being "full time", he wondered how he would pass the time all day. However, before they even got all the boxes unpacked, he realized that he had more than enough responsibilities to occupy him. There were hospital visits to make, shut-ins to visit, bulletin material to put together, committees to meet, and two sermons and a mid-week Bible study to prepare. It did not take but a few days to realize that his ministry at this church would not be as laid back as it had been in his earlier one.

It is customary that a pastor is paid as well as the average member of the church. In addition, any out-of-pocket expenses that he might incur should be reimbursed. His housing and utilities should be taken care of just like you take care of those items at the church. He should be provided with adequate health insurance and a fair figure should be deposited in your denominations Annuity or 401k program. A pastor cannot be paid too much because he does a lot that you do not know about, such as counseling the ideal couple in the church to help save their troubled marriage and late-night visits to the hospital or the death bed. This church set a good example in all these areas.

There was more organization, more people, and more structure in this new church. However, as John became more familiar with the people, he found that they had the same kind hearts, the same kind of love for his family, and, the same compassion, the same caring for lost souls. They finally got settled into the church home, which was a typical country house at the intersection of two gravel roads. One of the roads ran past the south side of the house and the other on the west side which was the front of the house. When they were kids, both John and Annie lived on gravel roads, so dust was nothing new to either of them. However, they did not have a clue about dust until they moved here. Anytime a car passed the house it was like being in a tsunami sand storm.

John discovered early on that this was a family congregation. Most of the members were related, either by birth or marriage. To top it off, the former pastor Brother James Twitty was also closely related to all of them. He was the brother of two of the deacons, one cousin was married to another of the deacons, his sister, another brother, and several cousins, as well as two of his children were also in the church. It was not long until intimidation flooded over John like another tsunami. The former pastor could open his Bible and in three minutes have an opening prayer, three alliterative points, a poem, and a death bed story, and preach it with deep conviction. John just knew that they would want to call the former pastor back after they heard a little more of John's preaching. As it turned out, that former pastor became a real "Barnabas" to John. He was a major source of encouragement and became one of John's best friends and remained so until his death. Intimidation transformed into security

As he tried to get adjusted in his new church, John thought he had really lost it. He would call on one of the men to pray and, instead of the man praying, his wife would pray. (I do not know why they felt they should do this, but they did it.) He thought they could surely understand him when they heard him say, "Brother so and so, will you lead us in this prayer?" While visiting one of the men's home, he finally asked what was happening. He told John how sacred prayer was to the families and that they just could not find words to express what they felt. They loved the Lord so much that they just could not talk to Him in public, they could not get their voices to cooperate. They honestly took Matthew 6:6-8 to heart. John decided he would rather have a handful of men who pray like these men than a church full of men that only prayed in public and never in secret.

John's former church had three deacons while this one had seven. These seven men, well at least six of them, were the most tender-hearted, godly men that John had ever been around. Their deacons' meetings were like small prayer meetings where these men silently poured their hearts out in expressing their worship of God.

These congregants came to love John's family and gave them a part of everything they grew in their gardens as well as regular invitations into their homes for a meal. Annie never bought an egg the whole time they were there. One of the men Russ in the community raised game roosters and sold them in the Philippines and shipped them there by plane. He. had lots of eggs that he had no use for, so guess who did have a use for them? His sister Maurice, who had never been married and never worked outside the home, was the housekeeper for this man and his brother, who also never married. The three of them lived together in the home where they were born. Maurice was an avid gardener and every year she would take the produce they did not eat or give away and would sell it in another one of her brothers' grocery store. That and a small government check was the extent of her income. Nevertheless, she donated the money she made selling her produce in the store to the special mission offerings.

Russ not only sold eggs, but he also sold chickens that he had no use for, so you could buy one for almost nothing. This is where John burned out on chicken. No matter who invited you to have a meal with them, they were going to serve some form of chicken. Now fifty years later John is convinced that you should never eat anything that does not have legs or lips. Chickens have no lips and John will not eat chicken to this very day. He ate enough chicken while serving that church to last him a lifetime. He felt sure that somewhere in the Bible it said, ***"Thou shalt not eat chicken"***. John used to say that it was found right next to the verse that says, ***"where there is love, there are biscuits"***.

Mark and Luke loved it there. The church was located by one of Mississippi's most attractive state parks, which provided the whole family with wonderful adventures. For the boys, there was a barn to play in and some neighbor kids Josh, Ken, and Charlie about a mile down the road. They were a little older than the Roberts' two boys, but they all enjoyed playing together. John and Annie's Volkswagen

Beetle became a source of entertainment. There was an elderly couple who had no way to get to church, so John, Annie, Mark, and Luke would go by to pick them up. Mark and Luke were always excited about that because there was no room for them in the car and they got to ride on the running board of the car. There was no one in the church that looked forward to Sunday any more than Mark and Luke, who was also amused that some people in town traveled by tractors instead of cars.

It is not unusual for church members to be generous to their pastor's family. But these folks were especially giving. Everything from a week's vacation in a condominium in Wyoming or Pigeon Forge, a visit with former members in Arizona, pottery, and plants. John's family also received plots. Not garden plots, but two beautiful cemetery plots! When the church voted to do this, one "friend" said he would be for it if John would go on and use it.

One of the most unusual gifts was a pig. A deacon named Cletus, whom John thought to be a friend and supporter, called and said, "Preacher, one of my sows had an unusual number of pigs, would you like to have one to fatten?" John said, "sure, we can fix up that place behind the pastorium and it will be the perfect place". They went to work on the pig pen that very day and made sure to do all they could to keep a small pig from getting out. When the enclosure was ready, Annie, Mark, and Luke were more delighted to see that pig than to see John when he came home. Cletus had brought the pig, took it out to the pen, looked it over and thought it would be alright. Well, it was alright for about two weeks. One day, the pig, whom they had named Ole Porkchop, escaped. John chased it until it got tired of running and stopped. Apparently, the pig thought they were playing. John was thinking of a heart attack. John and Annie reinforced the pen, put the pig back in and thought, he cannot get out now. But the next day the neighbor called, "pigs out". That went on until they took it to the meat processor.

John did not know how big the pig needed to be before having it processed. Someone said that it needed to have at least 100 pounds of processed meat. They could not figure out how to weigh the pig, but Annie came up with a brilliant idea. She suggested that they take the bathroom scale out to the pen, and John would weigh himself, then pick up the pig and calculate its weight. So, daily John would weigh himself, and then both together. This went on until John could no longer pick the pig up. Over the course of their ownership of this pig, John thought they must have chased him a hundred miles and fed him a thousand dollars' worth of feed. The deacon had assured them it was cheaper to raise your own meat than to buy it. Not true! They took Ole Pork Chop to the meat processor and two weeks later they were told that the pig was ready". The next night Annie prepared fresh vegetables and pork chops. As they sat down to eat, Mark or Luke one said, "Daddy, is this "Ole Pork Chop?" All four of them pushed the meat away and ate just the vegetables. They gave the rest of the meat away. After all, how could they eat something that they had held in their arms, looked deep into its eyes, and ran with it for miles?

CHAPTER SEVEN

Gardens, Banks, and Campers

One of the highlights of John's ministry in that church was the Sunday night when one of the older women brought her son's wife to services with her. He was in the army, stationed somewhere in South America where he got married to a Catholic woman and brought home to meet his family. When John gave the invitation at the close of his sermon, this woman came forward. She told John in halting English that she was Catholic, but said, "this is what I have been looking for all my life". She and John knelt by the front pew and she prayed, asking Jesus to come into her heart and life. That was one of the most meaningful times in John's ministry there.

John and Annie had their first garden while living there. They grew okra, tomatoes, beans, and all kinds of vegetables. They would use the early mornings to work in the garden. They only had one hoe, so they took turns using it in a losing battle to keep the weeds out. One of their members, Roy was a mail carrier and their road was among his earliest stops. Whenever he passed their house, it was just after John had set down to rest and Annie had the hoe. He never saw John contribute one minute's work in that garden. They worked hard but enjoyed every minute being together during those early morning hours.

John had two terribly difficult days at this church. One involved the pianist Kirby. He was a tremendously talented young man, who was attending college. He came home on weekends just to play for the church. On his way home one day, he was involved in an automobile accident that took his life. It absolutely rattled the whole church.

He and his talent meant so much to them and was deeply, deeply loved by the entire congregation. Kirby was a beautiful testimony for Christ.

The other tragic day also involved a death. One of the most beloved and respected deacons of the church, Lewis, suddenly dropped dead while on the job one day. John felt his absence profoundly; he had come to rely on him for counsel and advice. His presence was so felt in John's heart that one Sunday morning several weeks after his death, John called on him to pray. John was so embarrassed that he could have crawled under the pulpit.

One evening John received a call from a man in a city about fifty miles away. The man introduced himself and said he was calling on behalf of a pulpit committee from his church. He wanted to know if John would be willing to meet with their committee. John agreed, and they set a time to meet. John, Annie, and their sons arrived there filled with anxiety. The committee was waiting, and all the men introduced themselves and one by one, began to tell John about their church. After an hour or two of discussion, they invited John to come and preach a trial sermon. John told them he would pray about it and get back to them in a few days. Even though Mark and Luke were young, John and Annie always involved them in discussions that involved the family. After talking and praying about the matter, the decision was unanimous: they would go and preach the trial sermon.

This Chelebete, Mississippi church was just out of town and was at a major intersection of one of the main highways just a few miles from the State Line. The area seemed to be growing in that direction with subdivisions springing up on what would be the church field. It looked like a good opportunity for John and his family.

The two churches John had served to this point were sound, stable, and relatively trouble-free, but all of that may change if John, Annie, and the boys make their way to this new church. As it turned out, the whole area was a troubled area. This was in the days of Buford Pusser's reign as sheriff of the Tennessee county that joined the Mississippi county where the Roberts family would live. There was a lot of illegal activity that spilled over into the county and John would find this to be a challenging position.

John and Annie weighed the pros and cons of moving to another church at this time. Their oldest son had just started first grade and they did not want to uproot him. However, the more they talked and prayed, the more they felt the Lord leading them to this new church. They decided to just back their ears and go for it. A couple of Sundays later, John preached a trial sermon for them. Two weeks later the church voted on John to be their pastor. The vote was not unanimous this time, but a major percentage of the folk voted to call him. That Sunday afternoon, the chairman of the pulpit committee gave him the results of the vote and assured him that even though some did not vote for him it would be alright. They felt he was their man.

After considerable prayer, John called him back later in the week and said he would accept their call. The next Sunday John went through another heart-wrenching time telling their church that they were leaving to go elsewhere. There was something about this move that seemed like what a divorce must feel like. It was tough leaving these people. They had gained a warm place in their hearts and John and Annie hold them in high regard and have only fond memories to this day.

The Monticello Baptist Church moved the Roberts family. They sent two black men and a truck with sideboards on it that looked and smelled as if it had just come from a cattle sale. Sure enough, John found out later that it had. That should have thrown up a red flag, but they were too excited about moving to a new opportunity in a new town to let that deter them. The fact that this church was on the main highway close to the state line meant that a lot of people stopped by needing help of some kind. One couple came to John asking to be married. They were madly in love. John talked with them for a while and told them that he would have to pray about it and give it some thought. He decided that a Justice of the Peace would probably marry them anyway. So, John decided he would perform the marriage. After the ceremony, the new husband asked John what he owed him, John said, "Just what you feel it is worth", and the man gave him two dollars. Apparently, that was a true statement of its worth because three weeks later John read in the legal section of the local paper that they had filed for divorce.

Another time, a man and woman stopped by asking if John would marry them. The woman was pregnant. They talked a while and as it turned out it was a neighboring pastor and his wife just stopping by to introduce themselves. Needless to say, they left an indelible impression on John and Annie.

The first two churches John pastored were financially sound and spiritually grounded. Through the years, they had called out good deacons and other leaders to guide the course of the church. They did an excellent job of moving forward on a positive course. In addition, those churches had managed to seek out and call pastors who were good godly men that tried to glorify God and edify the people.

As John would learn, the new pastorate did not have leaders or members who had reached the same level of spiritual maturity as those in his former churches. The people were as good as gold but did not have the depth of understanding of the workings of a church yet. Would you want to take a guess as to what John's first official action as the pastor would be? You might think it would be to strengthen the Sunday School program, or the Discipleship Training program, or even have deacon training to help the deacons to understand their role in the growth of the church. No, it was none of those.

John could not believe it when the chairman of deacons called one day to ask if John would go with him to the bank. They rode to town together and the man never mentioned what the purpose of the bank visit was. As it turned out, the former pastor had led the church to build an educational building with twenty-one or twenty-two Sunday school classrooms. Far more rooms than they need even now, forty years later. Soon after the building was completed, the pastor moved. When the pastor, who was well loved, left, so did many of the people.

The church had borrowed the money to build those classrooms using the church-owned buildings and property as collateral. When the former pastor left, the offerings also took a nose-dive. The chairman of deacons wanted John to go to the bank with him to work out a solution to keep the bank from calling the note due. If that is not getting started by putting your best-negotiating foot forward, then I do not know what is.

They struggled financially for most of their ministry there. However, God blessed them immeasurably with souls saved and added members. As the church grew in number, it also grew financially, and the note was paid off before John left.

One time, Annie got in trouble that caused a little rift. One of the older boys and one of John's boys got into a shoving match after services one night. Well, it was a little more than a shoving match. Annie saw it and chastised the older boy. His mother Myrtis overheard and almost tore into Annie for reprimanding her kid. Over time the rift healed, and things got back to normal. John butted heads with the same family about another issue. They wanted to have a dance in the fellowship hall after one of the ball games. John sat down with this family and the deacons and said, "You can have a dance if you want to, but you will have it without me being your pastor". Another matter that took time to work through so that everyone was alright again.

It was not all trouble; they made some deep friendships. Several of the deacons had children the same age as theirs and they camped, fished, and ate at one another's house on Sunday nights after church. John learned over these fifty-five years that there are some places you can have your closest friends within the church family and some places you cannot. It worked well for them in this case, but it would not have worked at all in other places. One thing that John always made sure of was that everyone was treated the same. He did not show partiality to anyone.

One of these men, Eugene, was as country as a new barn door. When they were fishing, and it came time to eat, he could bait a worm on his hook, wipe his hands on his pants, and fix himself a bologna sandwich...and offer to fix you one. No one ever took him up on his hospitable offer.

Another man, a deacon named J.W, asked John, Annie, and the boys to go with them to Eureka Springs, Arkansas one fourth of July weekend to see the Passion Play. John did not know how to say "no." J.W., his wife and two kids, and John, Annie, and their two kids loaded up in the deacon's car and struck out for Arkansas. They drove most of the day getting there. John, Annie, and their boys rode in the back seat. The deacon and his wife both smoked. Not only does

Annie get car sick riding in back, but she also cannot stand cigarette smoke. The boys squirmed from the time they got in the car because they did not have the usual amount of room. At every rest area. John tried to get them to understand that everyone has a cross to bear and this was theirs for this weekend. It did not work. That night they went to the Passion Play. John could not stay awake as wonderful as it was, and Annie kept her head on her knees the whole time trying to keep from throwing up from being sick riding in the back seat. They spent the night and left for home early the next morning. Another day sandwiched in that car with the cigarette smoke. Finally arriving home, they talked about the trip and took an oath on their lives that they would never do that again. And, they have not.

While there, one of the deacons taught John to camp. They bought a tent and other items that would be needed for their first trip to the great outdoors. The first night at the State Park, they were in their sleeping bags sound asleep when somebody woke everybody up saying, "I'm wet". There was a terrible thunderstorm and water was running under the tent, which became ankle deep inside. Someone forgot to tell John how to set up a tent and prepare around it so that water could not run underneath. However, it did not deter the family. They finished out the night sleeping on some quilts that did not get wet.

One day, John was returning home from visiting the hospital in a neighboring city when he spotted a small camper with a For Sale sign on it. He stopped, looked at it, and decided that was what they needed. He went on home, told Annie about it, and they both went back to look at it the next day. It turned out that the camper had been involved in an accident. The insurance company paid off the claim and sold the camper to a person who repaired it. It was a good-looking little camper. You could not tell that it had been wrecked except it had no curtains and the cushions for the booth were gone. Annie said she could make some curtains and cushions if that was all it needed. So, they haggled a little bit with the owner and ended up buying it. They dragged that little camper all over the place with an old Plymouth station wagon. Camping was a good thing for the Roberts family; they camped with their sons as long as they were living at home. In fact, John and Annie camped well into their late seventies.

Remember, this church was located at a major intersection of two highways. Late one night there was a knock on the pastorium door. Annie went to the door and there stood a stranger, an intoxicated woman. She asked if they could take her home. Annie's first question was, "What are you doing out here this late at night?" The inebriated woman, as quick as a flash, said, "It wasn't this late when I started". Annie did not feel comfortable with John taking her home by himself. They both could not go because the boys were already asleep. So, Annie drove her and gave her a good lecture all the way there. Sadly, the woman was found dead behind one of the member's outbuildings a week later. She was intoxicated and died from exposure.

John learned a little about counseling while at this church because he was called upon to do so much of it. Everything from keeping the ideal couple from divorcing to young people who felt God was calling them into full-time ministry.

Overall, John had a good ministry there. He was still attending college while he was there and a church much closer to the school called him as pastor. They hated to leave their friends, but it looked like that was the way the Lord was leading. In later years, John helped with the funeral service of the husband and father of one of the families John, Annie and the boys felt closest to. In fact, Annie and Luke still stay in touch with the family to this day.

John had several pastor search committees to hear him, but this was the one that it seemed the Lord was leading John to. So, it was time for Annie to pack their things and hit the road again. They left all their churches with tears but looked forward with joy to the new opportunities.

CHAPTER EIGHT

Expectations

School was just starting when the Roberts family moved into the new church home.in Tunlaw, Mississippi. Luke and Mark were about 8 and 10 and loved it there because they were the new kids in town and made lots of friends easily. John and Annie did not adjust quite as fast as the boys did. As is usually the case, the pastor search committee did not give John the full history of the church. John began to discover that this "ideal church with no problems whatsoever" was not so ideal and trouble-free. This was a First Baptist church and the members were enormously proud of it. They had some strict expectations of their pastor. One was to visit prospects in certain parts of the town and leave the others alone. They expected him to wear a dark suit, dark shoes, a not-to-colorful tie, and walk through town and stop in at all the merchants. They wanted their members to have a certain standing in the community. John became very frustrated because he did not care which side of the tracks people came from as long as they would give their hearts to Jesus. It caused a little head-butting along the way.

John thought he was making some progress until one terrible day, one of the members from the other side of the track and her little two-year-old boy had been grocery shopping. Returning home, she parked the car and was taking groceries in the house while the little boy was still in the car. While she was still in the house, somehow the child knocked the car out of park and the car began to roll. The child fell out and the car rolled over him and killed him. The family was grief-stricken, and John spent a lot of time with them before, during, and after the funeral and burial.

Another member, Mrs. Clarkson commented to John that the bereaved family was surprised that the church did not send flowers. He told her that he was sure they did, but he would check on it. One of the more vocal and more haughty ladies, Mrs. Alluppity handled sending flowers when a death occurred in the church family. John stopped by her house on the way home and asked her about it. She was quite huffy and said, "No, I didn't send flowers, he was not a member". (They had just sent flowers to Hawaii the week before when a cousin of hers died.) John said, but the child's parents *are* members, so we need to send flowers to the home. She said, "I resent being told what to do. So, if that is the way it is going to be, I will just resign all my positions". John could only imagine how this was going to go over with the church since they were accustomed to her running about everything.

John told her that if she felt she needed to resign he would be glad to present her resignation to the church but send flowers to the home. Following that encounter, things went downhill. The church met for the midweek service in the fellowship hall. From the time John and Mrs. Alluppity squabbled, she would sit in the back of the fellowship hall every Wednesday night and rattle papers while John was trying to speak. John knew that he would never be effective there again, so he began to tell friends that he needed to move.

In the meantime, the president of the local bank Mr. Jackson - who was also a member of the church - had his secretary call John one day and ask him to drop by to see him. John went by that afternoon wondering which shoe was going to fall this time. He and Mr. Jackson engaged in a little small-talk until he finally got around to what he wanted to discuss. The banker said, "Pastor, I have come into a little money unexpectedly. I have paid my tithe on it but still have a little extra. I know that you must have some debt for your schooling. Would it embarrass you, or hurt your feelings if I paid that debt off?" John could not believe his ears and assured the man that it would do neither and he would be incredibly grateful. John tried to believe that this was the reason the Lord led him to this church because it sure did relieve quite a financial burden from the Roberts family.

Every Monday morning John met with a neighboring pastor and the associational missionary at a little coffee shop for fellowship. John told them about his discontent and asked them to pray with him about it. Every week they assured him they were praying for him and the situation. John felt pretty discouraged about leaving; he had been there just a little over a year. He felt that somehow, he had failed the Lord and the church. But there are times when you just cannot fight the authorities, and you might as well accept it.

In a few weeks, there was a pastor search committee coming from a church in another state. This was in the day when you did not know that a search committee was coming to hear you. He preached for them, had several meetings with their committee, and waited hopefully for a call from the committee. John and the family went for a trial sermon and had to wait two weeks for them to vote on him. About mid-afternoon on Sunday, the committee Chairman called and said the church had voted to call him. John did not have to wait and pray about this one, he and Annie had been praying for weeks. He told the committee that he would accept their call.

This was the only time John and Annie were glad to leave a church. His ministry seemed to be at a standstill. The church seemed cold and indifferent to the lost and to each other. The deacons' meetings seemed like torture sessions to John. What a difference there was between these men and the deacons in the other churches he had served!

John learned a lot from his experiences at this church. He learned that all deacons were not men of pure hearts; he learned that everyone was not as anxious to meet the needs of their pastor family as others, and he learned that what you see in and hear from a person on Sunday does not necessarily carry over to Monday through Saturday. John learned one other especially important lesson: every experience, the good as well as the bad, prepares you for what lies ahead. So, once again Annie began packing up their belongings and got ready to leave what friends they had and move to a new church in Tennessee.

The church sent a moving van for the Roberts' belongings. This made the move so much easier than the moves they had made up to that time. The members had an old-fashioned "pounding" planned for them, welcoming them to their new church ever so graciously with food and festivities. Each family member had a different reaction to their new home. Mark and Luke, now 11 and 13 were thrilled to be there. They had kids close to their age that lived on either side of them. Annie was delighted because they had just finished completely remodeling the church home. John was anxious because this was the largest church he had pastored so far.

John's apprehension soon dissipated as he came to know the people better, especially as he spent time with the deacons. They were a godly group of men that loved the Lord and loved the church and wanted to see anybody and everybody saved. They were men that came from a variety of professions and were very progressive in their thinking. They may have questioned in their minds most things that John suggested. But even if they had tried it before and failed, they were willing to give it another try.

One of the deacons who was also a member of the pulpit committee asked John one day, "Do you remember that pastor you prayed with about moving and he assured you that he was praying that the Lord would open a door of opportunity for you somewhere?" John said, "Yes, I remember him. He was a good friend". The deacon said, "Well, while he was praying with you, he was trying to get this church for himself. He had a friend that talked with us several times encouraging us not to call you but to call your friend". It was at that point that John learned that not only can you not trust some people, there are also some pastors that you cannot trust either.

It was here that John and Annie began an annual Christmas dinner for the deacons and their wives. It was one of the best things they could have done because it was at these dinners that all of them learned to appreciate each other more deeply. The deacons and John did not always agree completely on every little thing, but they learned to continue praying and talking through it until they came to a mutual understanding. Things always seemed to work out for the glory of God.

Chapter Nine

Fish and Fire

Annie was truly fortunate, as there was a Vocational School not too far from where they now lived. She enrolled in a Bookkeeping/Accounting program and loved every minute of it. Not long after she graduated, one of the men in the church who was on the board of a Federal Credit Union told her about an opening at the Credit Union. She applied for the job and got it. She did a wonderful job and gradually began to move up. When they left, she had reached the point of being the Credit Union's Office Manager.

One other thing about this new church. They were some of the most kind, generous, loving people John had met. The entirety of John's pastorate there, Annie never had to buy a single outfit. Mrs. Dugood kept Annie dressed in the finest clothes. Far better than John could afford to buy for her. John often remarked that he did not believe the lady never cared one thing about him. She never bought John anything, but she was a breath of fresh air to Annie.

The church was only a couple of miles from the Tennessee River and Mark and Luke spent their spare time on the river bank fishing. Those boys lived in the woods, hunting everything from rabbits to deer, and on the river bank fishing for any kind of fish that would bite a hook. It was through their experiences there that they learned how to be true survivors and providers. Luke killed his first deer while there. An elderly gentleman named Daniel, who was lost but attended church, taught him how to dress and cut up a deer as good as any butcher could. In fact, both Mark and Luke killed their first deer there.

It was here that the boys became involved in all kinds of sports. They became quite good, especially at baseball and basketball. It was also here that they found their first girlfriends. It has been about forty years since the Roberts moved to their next church, but John, Annie, Mark, and Luke still consider those rolling hills and rushing river as home. This is the first place where they made lifelong friends. One of their playmates, a little girl named Abby lived next door. She was as cute as a button and as tough as a pine knot. She could hold her own with any of the kids in the neighborhood. She had two older brothers that were past the playmate stage. However, Mark and Luke still care deeply for all three of them and consider them friends to this day.

Several years later Daniel, the old gentleman who helped Luke and Mark dress his deer, trusted Christ as Savior and John had the privilege of baptizing him. John was fortunate in that he baptized several adults while at this church.

One couple that John led to accept Christ as savior was Gomer and Gertrude, an elderly couple who were both lost. John won the man to the Lord just before he died. His wife was on oxygen and could hardly breathe. The wife rarely came to church but got sick enough that she began to worry about her own demise. On Sunday when she made her profession of faith, her daughter had to help her down the aisle. John was afraid to baptize her because he thought sure holding her breath would kill her. However, she made it, and everyone was happy that she did. A few weeks after her baptism, John and Annie ran into her and a gentleman in a store in town. She was walking fine and no longer had to have oxygen. John never did figure out if it was his baptizing or the new man that healed her. They laugh about that to this day.

After being there a couple of years, John proposed that the church build a fellowship hall that would accommodate the people. A building committee was elected and after much prayer and many revisions to the original plan, the church voted to go ahead with the building. It was a much-needed addition and the people were extremely proud of it. Every church John pastored, except one, needed to do some kind of building and this one was the easiest.

The Roberts continued to enjoy outdoor camping, and this church was in the area where they did most of their camping. So, they sold the camper. John and Annie had talked for months about buying a boat but had never come to a firm decision. John had a revival back in Mississippi and was telling the pastor how much they wanted a boat. As luck would have it, the pastor's son had a boat that he never used and would love to sell it. He and John rode over to his son's house one day to look at this boat. It was sitting under a pecan tree, covered in tree sap, had not been moved in years, and it had been even longer than that since the motor had been cranked. John always was an easy touch and he bought the boat. When the revival was finished on Friday, night John left for home.

The next morning before breakfast he told Annie to look at what had followed him home. She saw that boat and burst into tears worse than if there had been a death in the family. She cried all day long. At one point she asked John how much he had paid for it and he told her, and she had another intense crying spell. John did not know if she might kill him or divorce him, but he was afraid that one or the other might happen.

In days to come, she became reconciled and the whole family began working on that boat, repairing the things that were broken or worn out and scrubbing the boat inside and out trying to get off the tree sap. They worked for weeks, almost every day trying to make the boat look presentable. Washed and polished, it looked like a new boat. However, when they took it to the lake, the motor would not start. John took it to a marine repair shop, and they had to rebuild the engine, which was quite expensive. When he told Annie how expensive, she had another crying spell. Of course, with what John had invested in the boat, he could have bought a new one. While they were at the First Baptist Church Pocono, they taught about every kid there how to ski. That boat, as much grief as it caused, was one of the best investments in family life that John could have made because it drew them all closer.

There are multiple demands in ministering to a church family. It took John time to realize that his congregants were not going to love him anymore or any less if he took a day or two off each week. His family appreciated that he did this on a consistent basis and this freedom made John an even better pastor.

Just as Paul seemed to love some churches more than others, John and his family loved this church more than any of the others he pastored. Maybe it was because of the consideration given to his whole family. At Christmas, for example, the church always gave John an extremely generous monetary gift. Even more meaningful was the fact that almost every member gave Annie, Mark, and Luke their own gift. They also gave John a generous raise every year. There was never a question about it; it was something the church family wanted to do and did it with joy while some of the churches John pastored seemed to resent giving him any salary increase at all. It was not the gifts or the raises that caused John and his family to love them so, it was the spirit in which it was given. They had hearts willing to give.

The church had many teens and John enjoyed taking them on trips and to conferences. A considerable number was baptized while John was there. Only one girl, Millie, ever gave John any problem. Her morals were not becoming a Christian, but John kept working with her. One incident – involving Mark – seemed to have a positive effect. Millie invited him to go to some function with her. Mark did not want to go but did not know how to decline, So John told him to tell her that he would not let him go. Would you believe that girl came to the house and wanted to know why John would not let Mark go? John told her the truth that her poor reputation was the reason and if she did not change, Mark could not go anywhere with her. It made her mad for a while, but it seemed that her behavior gradually improved and she got over being angry.

There were four or five families that took John and Annie under their wings and through their advice and counsel, John became an effective pastor and better preacher. It is always special to learn from your church family. They socialized regularly in one another's homes after services and all became remarkably close. One of these men, Curtis, asked John if he remembered the neighboring pastor who met for prayer with him at his former church and John said yes. Curtis told him that while that pastor was praying with you to get this church, he was working behind the scenes trying to get it himself. It was another lesson that John learned. Just as every member is not always what they appear to be, neither are pastors. Since that time,

John has not fully entrusted any pastor with the deep things that troubled him.

One of John's deacon, Roger, was an avid fisherman. He taught John how to fish the river for White Catfish. The main river channel was 50-60 feet deep in places and you could float down the channel bouncing your bait off the bottom of the river bed and catch a fish almost every time you dropped your bait. Roger said the fish was a white color because they stayed so deep in the water. John and his family often went in their boat to fish the river, and they all became exceptionally good fishermen. They still enjoy fishing today and go to a State Park lake and fish for channel cats every chance they get. It is rare for them to come home without a mess of fish.

John volunteered for the community fire department. They got a fire call one day, and John and one other were all that turned out. He and his friend fired up the old 1942 LaFrance open cab firetruck. With a tank full of water, it would not go over 35 miles an hour. They made it to the fire and discovered that the mother was outside her burning trailer, hanging up clothes to dry. When she turned to go back in, her little baby was inside. The fire was so intense she could not reach the baby. It was one of the saddest days of John's ministry.

On a much lighter note, the volunteers always teased the fire chief about a mistake he had made one night. The chief, Jake, was out in his yard and saw a huge orange glow coming from an area near the lake where a lot of cabins were situated. His first thought was a cabin fire. He sounded the alarm and took off in the firetruck by himself. When he got to the point where he could better see that orange glow, it turned out to be the moon rising over the lake. The other men never let him live that down. Another humorous story they told about Jake was one night when a slip that housed a lot of boats at the marina caught fire. Again, the chief jumped in the firetruck and took off. Firetrucks from a neighboring station were already there when he arrived and were parked several feet back from the slip. But as Jake came roaring down the hill, he ran past the crowd that had gathered, ran past the other firetrucks, and finally stopped just feet from the fire. He jumped out and began to put water on the flames. When it was extinguished, one of the neighboring firefighters asked why he got so close to the flames. His response was, "I've been meaning to have the brakes fixed on that old truck".

There was a paper mill located in the area where John lived. When other pastors found out where John pastored, they would ask how he could stand the smell of that paper mill. John always responded with an answer he had heard from one of the men who worked there, "It smells like bacon and eggs to me".

John and his family were friends with an Evangelist and his team. They were going to hold a crusade in the area in a few weeks. John had been witnessing to Mr. Pitney, an unsaved man, for several months. They became good friends primarily because of John's interest in his hobby. He was a knife maker and John spent some time asking about his trade. One day, Mr. Pitney's wife was taken to the hospital and John visited with them while she was there. He always witnessed to the man before he left, but to no avail.

Mrs. Pitney came home from the hospital and one Wednesday just before prayer meeting John got a call that her husband had died. John felt like *he* would die because he just knew that Mr. Pitney went into eternity unsaved. John rushed over to the house where several friends had already gathered there. John went in and asked where Mrs. Pitney was, and a neighbor answered, "they have already taken her". Suddenly John realized that it was not the husband, but his wife who had died. As sad as it was, John felt relieved as he offered words of comfort and witnessed to him again. Mr. Pitney attended the Evangelistic crusade one night and was gloriously saved; John had the privilege of baptizing him. He was active in the church and made a beautiful pocket knife for John, which he still carries in his pocket from time to time.

The Evangelistic team was busy with meetings and asked John to visit a county in Georgia to do the counselor training for an upcoming crusade there. John was thrilled at the opportunity to do so and to learn about a new culture. Upon arriving, John met with the Associational Missionary and they worked out all the details. Fifty men and women took part in counselor training with John. About two weeks after the crusade ended, John and Annie received an early-morning phone call and a voice asked, "How do you get to Pocono, Tennessee?" John gave directions and a couple of weeks later a pulpit committee from the Georgia church showed up. It was a rainy, dreary day, attendance was down, and John felt like he preached one of his worst sermons ever. The committee met with John after the service that day and invited him to preach a trial sermon at their church. John told them that he would let them know before the following Sunday.

There was a lot to consider; it would be further away from family; it was not the right time for Mark and Luke who were in a high school; things were going well at the church, and John was working on his master's degree. But as they prayed about the matter, it seemed that God was opening another door of opportunity. So, John told them that before he preached, he wanted to meet with as many members as could come and just talk about the church, John's style of preaching, and other details.

CHAPTER TEN

On the Road, Again

It was only a couple of weeks before John and the family had planned to go to Gatlinburg for a brief vacation. John thought he could kill two birds with one stone, so he contacted the pulpit committee and planned to meet them on a Saturday morning. The time came for the family trip and they spent the night in a town near the church where John was to meet with about fifty people. John learned a lot in the meeting, such as the former pastor was asked to leave; it was a Southern Baptist Church, but pretty much in name only; and the church had a reputation as being troubled and running off preachers. John felt the Lord's leadership so strongly that he let none of those things trouble him. He agreed to come back in two weeks and preach a trial sermon. They went on to Gatlinburg and had an enjoyable time, but John could not get the church off his mind and the family began to prepare to spend the weekend with this prospective church.

The day finally arrived and John, Annie and the boys made their way to Walkertown, where the church had arranged for them to stay. John's sermon intentionally revealed some important things about himself. He wanted them to know that he was committed to the Principles and Programs of the Southern Baptist Convention and expected that same commitment from the church. He believed in the Mission Program and offerings that were promoted through the Foreign Mission Board and the Home Mission Board. Overall, it was a good day and two good services.

The following Sunday afternoon one of the committee members called and said the church voted to call John. It was not unanimous, but as they put it, it was a good call for them. The fellow went on explaining and that the "no" votes came from the older ladies' Sunday School class, but it would not be a problem. Later, John would find out that the class was a dedicated supporter of the "PTL Club". The women were disturbed by John's emphasis on Southern Baptist Missions. Now John and the family have a decision to make. John felt led to go, Annie said she would support him wherever he was. Luke, the younger son did not have much to say about it, but Mark did not want to go. This is where all his friends were, he was a senior, and he liked it there. But, what else could he do besides go along with his father's decision?

So, the decision was made to accept the church call. The hardest thing John had done to this point was to announce his decision to his present church the following Sunday. He gave them a thirty-day notice - it was the longest thirty days of his life. The new church got a moving company to come in and pack everything and deliver all the furnishings. They were leaving the place that all of them considered home and were leaving the state again. It was scary going to a place where you did not know one single soul. John felt like a missionary moving to a foreign country. The culture, mindset, personalities, and even the language was different.

Situated in the mountains of Georgia, the people had a mountain mentality and were deeply rooted in tradition. The people were fiercely independent; they believed that if it had been done that way for the past one-hundred-years, it should be done the same way for the next one-hundred years. This mindset was to be found throughout the community, but nowhere any greater than in the churches. Also, if you were not born and raised there you were always an outsider.

John and Mark came ahead of the moving van. They pulled the boat behind a car loaded with much of the family clothing and John and Mark sandwiched in. It was about a six-hour trip, so they left early in the morning. John did not want to pull that boat over the mountains after dark. Annie and Luke would follow the next day. Now, everything that they had just removed from one house had to be unpacked and organized in another house, which was no small task, as every minister knows. The first night there, John and Mark went to Wednesday night prayer meeting. This would be John's first service in the new church, and it was the night for the church business meeting. That is no big deal, except they were voting on a salary increase that John and the committee had agreed on. John was a little nervous, but everything went more smoothly than John had feared.

One of the committee men, Roscoe, came and asked John if he could take Mark to the high school, as they were just beginning football practice. Mark and Luke played every sport that was available to them and excelled in some of them. Of course, John told him he could, and that left John alone with all these people that he did not know, and his oldest child had just been taken away to go to a school that John did not even remember how to get there. The prayer/business meeting was over, John found the school and picked Mark up. Furthermore, they spent their first night in this strange new town in the local motel, without Annie and Luke. The next day Annie and Luke arrived and so did the moving van.

About mid-morning of the second day, one of the deacons visited. John thought how nice of him to come by to check on them. That was true, but there was more to it. One of the members of the church had just died and the deacon wanted to take John to their home to offer a little comfort to the family. John thought, "Boy, talk about hitting the ground running". They courteously asked John to have a part in the funeral service. He just hoped that in his cluttered new house he could find a suit. It seems that marked the beginning of what would be a stressful ministry. They were not bad days; it just seemed that they were rushed days.

The church put a picture of John's family in the county newspaper, along with a little information about the family. The story included some background information about John. They had not been in Jeffries, Georgia long before one of the State service agencies asked John if he would counsel some of their clients occasionally. John was one of those people, as was true of all the family, who could not say no or did not know when to say no. However, this gave John an opportunity to witness to some people that he would never have met had it not been for the social service agency. In fact, unbeknownst to the church, they gained several new members because of those counseling sessions. Of course, the church was never made aware of John's connection with them.

Within a couple of weeks after arriving, Annie got a job at one of the local banks. That was wonderful, except it really slowed down the process of getting things in order in their new home. Annie worked as a teller and, of course, all the customers wanted to know who she was. When she told them who she was and that her husband was pastor of With Hope Baptist Church they would laugh and say, "well he won't be there long, they will run him off". That bothered them at first; they did not know whether to unpack or not. It also bothered them that the church had that kind of reputation. John and Annie worked hard to do things in the community that might change the way people thought about the church. Gradually the church's reputation did take a turn for the better. John became a respected figure in the community and in the Association of Churches.

Mark never did make a clean break from their former home. He was unhappy for a long time but finally accepted the situation as he got involved in the high school's football program. One night he took a hit and tore his knee. He was transported to the local hospital and in short order, they sent him to a trauma center in a neighboring town. The ER doctor examined him and said the knee would be sore, but he could resume his activities. In one of the following games, Mark was injured again, so John and Annie took him to an orthopedic surgeon the next day. After the surgeon's examination, he told John and Annie that "I don't see how the kid could walk; his knee was so bad". Sadly, that ended his football career.

Luke decided not to play ball instead, of all things, he got into High School Rodeo as a bull rider. John let him do that with one stipulation. Pray before he got on the bull and - if he felt uneasy - let them open the gate and turn the bull out. I think Luke only turned the bull out one time. He progressed from bull riding to calf roping. John bought him a horse and Luke traveled all over Georgia roping calves.

Mark and Luke both got jobs at a local grocery store owned by one of the deacons. The boys gained a lot of respect in the community as they took groceries to people's cars. Both were hard workers, well-liked and treated kindly. Nevertheless, it was stressful for John and Annie raising two action-packed teenagers. Meanwhile, the church, with great reservation, began to move in the direction John felt that they should go. The older women's Sunday School class reluctantly began to lend more support to Southern Baptist missions and gradually gave up their support of the PTL program. The PTL club was an organization that supposedly did ministry work. However, the head of it, Jim Baker was arrested for embezzlement and the ministry was pretty much shut down. Some resented John leading them out of this, but when the PTL Scandal broke they were glad that they were no longer part of such a ministry.

The Sunday School class also began to do a turn-around and became the best friends and best supporters John and Annie had. Annie would coordinate trips for the senior adults. Every year around Labor Day, John and Annie would take a van load of them to the mountains to a pick-your-own apple orchard. John drove the van and it filled with seniors and apples. John used to tell them "if we have a wreck, all they will find is apple sauce". They enjoyed these trips so much that Annie began to coordinate overnight trips to the mountains. She would make deals with motels and restaurants, figure up how much the trip would cost for gas, lodging, and meals and calculate a per person cost. John and Annie made some life-long friends on these little excursions.

John worked hard to try to help the church grow. His efforts paid off in having new people join. In time, the church became one of the strongest churches in the Association of Churches. Some did not always agree with John and resisted his efforts, sometimes fiercely. However, the disagreements usually worked themselves out over time.

The church sanctuary was not arranged well and was outdated. John suggested a remodeling project that called for a complete renovation of the sanctuary along with new pews. John and the deacons discussed the matter for a while and finally agreed to recommend it. They had plans drawn up and received bids on the costs. Having all the information in hand, the deacons presented it to the church. There was a lot of discussion and disagreement at first, but the church voted, the recommendation passed. The remodeling took several weeks, but when it was finished it seemed that almost every member was proud of the fresh look.

The church had a small fellowship area and was in desperate need of more space. Several years after the remodeling, John recommended that the church build a large fellowship hall with bathrooms and a large kitchen. A building committee formed, and they began to work on plans. As the committee met to work on the details, one of the members, Justin, would get upset, resign from the committee, and leave the meeting. That went on the entire time the committee met. However, he was always back for the next meeting. Finally, a contractor was hired to draw up plans and a bidding process began. The contractor who did the remodeling of the sanctuary got the bid and soon they were moving dirt, getting ready for the much-needed space. Every member of the church was glad to see the building completed.

Pete, one of the deacons, made a proposal that would save the church some money as it paid for the new building. He offered to loan the church the money at a nominal interest rate, then donate the interest back to the church. This saved thousands of dollars and made the payments low enough that they did not put the church in a financial bind.

During this time, the church needed to call a full-time Minister of Music and Youth Worker. They found a young man who was a good fit for the position. In addition to his salary, the church was going to give him a monetary allowance for housing. Before he moved on the church field Joyce, one of the ladies in the church invited John and Annie to her house. She had recently lost her husband to a heart condition. She and her son were there when John and Annie arrived. [name]Joyce said that she had a piece of land across the street from her house and she wanted to give it to the Roberts' to build a house on. After John got over the shock, he told her that they could not accept her gift as great as it was, but they insisted. John finally told her that the only way he could accept it was that if he did not build a home on the property within a year, the property would revert to her. They agreed, and John and Annie just floated home they were so excited.

So, John met with the deacons and told them he wanted to build a house. He asked if they would be willing to let the new Music Director live in the church home and give John the housing allowance that they were going to give him. Surprisingly, they voted to recommend it and the church voted unanimously in favor of the recommendation.

John and Annie arranged for financing at the local bank, had a reputable builder to dry it in, and over the next six months, they learned how to build a house. They hardly knew how to drive a nail, much less build a house. Some contractor friends gave them helpful tips. However, when they came to a dead end and needed more help, they went to a neighboring town where a subdivision was being built. They would drive through until they saw a house that was about to the completion point of their house. John would go in, talk to the carpenters, tell them what they were trying to do, and the carpenters would tell John what they needed. They would even take a piece of scrap lumber and draw a diagram. The carpenters would laugh but were glad to help. This process went on until John and Annie finished the house …three days before the bank's deadline. They were blessed by the help of friends who gave them money, labor, and discounts. The house was truly a labor of love from people in the whole community.

CHAPTER ELEVEN

Leukemia, Lymphoma, or Lupus?

About this time, John and Annie were raking leaves and John became so exhausted that he had to sit down and lean up against a tree. Annie was afraid he had a heat stroke. But the fatigue did not go away, and Annie took him to a doctor who said, "Oh, you just need a little rest and a good night's sleep". He gave him a prescription and sent him home. Whatever the prescription was, it made John feel crazy; he just could not take it. The extreme fatigue would not let up, so Annie took him back to the doctor, who became more concerned. The doctor did some tests and blood work and had them wait to get some preliminary results. In a few minutes, the doctor came back and told John that he had arranged for him to be admitted into the hospital. There, John had other exams, x-rays, and all kinds of tests. After several days in the hospital, the doctor said, "Mr. Roberts, you have an aggressive form of leukemia. You need to go home and get your affairs in order because you will not live long." You could have cut the air with a knife because the shock was so thick. John was forty-three years old, he did not have to make plans to die, he has already made them.

The doctor went on to tell John to make an appointment with an oncology group in Atlanta, but it was three months before he could get an appointment. During these weeks of waiting, John tried to keep up his activity at church. However, when he would finish his sermon on Sunday, he was so fatigued he could hardly get back to the car. When John saw the oncologist, he found an enlarged lymph node under John's right arm. He told him that he had lymphoma and they needed to remove the node to see if it was Hodgkin's or Non-Hodgkin's. While John was recovering from that surgery, the doctors decided to perform a liver biopsy. The surgeon came into John's hospital room and a nurse administered a localized anesthetic injection. After the doctor had the biopsy sample, he said, "Son, I hate to tell you this, but I missed your liver; I'm going to have to try again". By this time John was hurting so badly that sweat was pouring off him like he had just come out of the shower. Finally, the doctor agreed to administer pain medication and got the necessary liver tissue successfully. John had to remain laying on his side for an hour. He hurt between his shoulder blade as though someone had hit him with an axe. The lymph node and the liver biopsies both came back with nonspecific results. The oncologist told John they would just monitor him for a few weeks. John came back home still so fatigued he could hardly stand in the pulpit. This went on for several months. No better, no worse.

They finally sent John to an infectious disease doctor who told him he had lupus. He went from dying with leukemia to lymphoma to lupus. John would tell people that he was expecting to get a Lincoln or Lexus any day now. But finally, there was a new diagnosis: chronic fatigue syndrome. This was in the day when most doctors did not believe that was a valid illness. John had to drive the one-hundred miles to Atlanta every week for fifty-two weeks for injections. John showed some improvement but reached a ceiling that he could never break through. Thirty-five years later, John did develop lymphoma. The disease was in his bone marrow and in polyps in his colon. His oncologist told him that it could have been in remission for all those thirty-five years. John still struggles with chronic fatigue but manages to do what he must do. He had two different rounds of chemotherapy that really put him flat on his back for a while. He still has lymphoma but, thankfully, is in full remission again.

John and Annie stayed at this church known for running preachers off for almost seventeen years. During that time, several pastor-search committees approached John about becoming their pastor, but he never felt that he could leave the Church. Until one day, John received a call from the chairman of a search committee in Mississippi. From the moment they began to talk, John felt that this was the place God wished him to be. As providence would have it, John had a revival scheduled in about two weeks about fifty miles from this church in Mississippi. An agreement was reached that the committee would come one night during the revival to hear John and to talk with him. After the service, they all went back into the fellowship hall and spent about two hours discussing the matter. John agreed to come to their church and preach a trial sermon. So, John and Annie drove the distance and arrived at the Motel the church had arranged for them to stay on Friday night. On Saturday, they spent the day looking over the church field and the church. That night the committee members, their spouses, and John and Annie all went to a restaurant and talked about the prospects and possibilities the church offered. This was the most honest and straightforward committee John had ever dealt with. John and the committee members seemed excited about the possibility of John becoming their pastor. John was, too.

John preached that Sunday as if he was preaching to his own church. The people were pleasant, and a number of the members told John that they hoped the church would call him to be their pastor. After a brief meeting with the committee following the service, John and Annie traveled back home to Georgia. The two of them really wanted to go to this church – it was a small-town church with lots of potentials. The church had been without a pastor for several months and was anxious to get a pastor. John and Annie were anxiously awaiting the church's decision.

The following Sunday, John had the strangest feeling; he did not feel that he belonged in his current church any longer. He felt that he should be at the [name] Goose Pond Baptist church in Mississippi. It made preaching difficult with his body present but his heart and mind nearly four hundred miles away. When the phone rang, John's heart almost stood still knowing that it was the committee chairman. The voice on the other end of the line said, "Well preacher, are you ready to move to Mississippi? The church overwhelmingly voted to extend a call to you". John finally took a breath as he told the man that he would accept their call and would move in thirty days. The chairman said they would arrange a moving company. The following Sunday John gave his church a thirty-day notice. This was the first time in all his years as a pastor that John felt no remorse about leaving. He knew that after almost seventeen years in this church it was time for him to leave.

John and Annie's oldest son, Mark married a girl from the church, Hazel. A couple of years after their wedding they had a little girl, Hope. She was the apple of her daddy's eye. A few years after Hope was born her mother left them. Mark and Hazel got a divorce and Mark gained custody of Hope. He did all a human could do to raise her right. Mark and Hope lived on in the house they were living in when he and Hazel divorced for a while. It was so hard being a single parent that he and Hope moved in with John and Annie. Annie reverted to her child-rearing days and both John and Annie enjoyed every minute of having them with them. All the teachers praised Mark for his attentiveness to Hope and involvement in the various organizations at school. Hope is grown now, and Mark has married again and is on disability due to four different strokes that left him completely without feeling anywhere on his body. They told him he would never walk but he proved them wrong. He walks, drives, and does fine except for a tremor.

Luke bought some land in a neighboring town. He wanted to put a mobile home on it. John was helping him clean off a ditch bank one day and he said he was going to run to the store and get them something to drink. John waited…and waited…and waited. Luke finally got back and come to find out he had met a girl at the store that he had been flirting with while John was doing all that waiting. As it turned out, she liked him as well as he did her and they married. A couple of years later they had a little girl, Christal. She was so tiny and looked so fragile that John was afraid to hold her. Then, a couple of years later they had a little boy, Lance. They too were the apples of their daddy's eye. Christal, of course, is grown now and has the two sweetest, most precious children since Hope, Cristal, and Lance was born. A little boy, Timothy that is small like his mother is, and Grace, who is another living doll. She and Timothy always demand your undivided attention. The only problems John and Annie had concerning moving to their new church was leaving their children and grandchildren. Of course, Timothy is also grown, has graduated from college and lives and works in Alabama. He went to college on a band scholarship. While the band was on a trip to Hawaii, he met the prettiest young woman, Ruth. They plan to be married in the summer. John will have the pleasure of marrying them. John had the privilege of baptizing and marrying his children and grandchildren.

The thirty days that John and Annie waited to move passed slowly, although they were incredibly sad to leave their children and grandchildren. This was the first move they had made when all four of the family members were not involved. John cried all the way to the Mississippi state line.

When John, Annie, and the moving van arrived at their new home the yard was filled with church members waiting to help unload the furniture. That was a first in their many years of ministry.

CHAPTER TWELVE

The Best is Yet to Be

John and Annie wondered why the Lord took them all the way back so close to where they were raised. During the first several months there, John and Annie began to lose family members in death. Annie's father became ill and was hospitalized nearby, so Annie could visit him often. One Easter Sunday morning, she felt a need to go to the hospital. While Annie was out of the room her father told a nurse that he was going to die that day. She said, "oh, no, you're getting better, you're not going to die". A brief time later he went into cardiac arrest and died. It was some consolation that Annie was close enough to where he lived that she could spend more time with him than since she married.

That was not all the sadness for the Roberts family. While they were at this Mississippi church, John's stepfather died, his stepmother and mother all died. However, as with Annie and her dad, John got to spend time with all of them that he could not have if he had remained in Georgia.

While at this church, John and Annie made more lifelong friends. John and the deacons were especially close. Usually, the deacons want the pastor to work out any problems that arise within the church. However, at the first deacons' meeting, they told John, "If you have a problem, or if you hear of one, you tell us and we will take care of it, we don't want you to be embroiled like that." John wondered if this was for real or just talk, but it was genuine. These deacons were masters at handling potential problems that undoubtedly arise in every church.

Annie began having some unusual heart palpitations and made an appointment with a cardiologist. After extensive tests, her doctor determined that she needed to have a pacemaker. They set up a stress test which she was unable to complete. That called for more extensive tests and they set up an appointment for a heart cath. Annie really dreaded this and was quite anxious about it. Following this, her doctor sent her to an Electro-cardiologist for the pacemaker. When he went over all the tests, he said that he thought the problem could be fixed with medication. It turned out to be a mitral valve prolapse which they could treat with medication.

There was a service station/restaurant/old men's hangout on the highway. John began going there most mornings to drink coffee with the men. There were about a half dozen regulars. Slowly, every one of those men started coming to church and most of them eventually joined. Something very unusual happened the day Annie's heart Cath was scheduled. One of the men, a retired Air Force Colonel, who has gone on to be with the Lord, called together the service station employees, the cooks, and the waitress, everyone sitting around the table and anyone else in the place and had a prayer for Annie. He gave John a copy of the prayer. Following is a copy:

> *It is a beautiful day to rejoice. Frontiers were crossed this morning.*
>
> *At 7:45 in an establishment more dedicated to the serving of mammon, Budweiser and Nashville musicians, customers and cooks alike entered their prayer closets to pray for the Well-being of Sister Annie Roberts who was given a fright last week when a cardiac stress test was aborted pending this morning's 7:45 am procedure.*
>
> *I expect the prayers went something like this at least mine did:*
>
> *Precious Savior, Heavenly Father, Gentle Comforter, this assembly joins with individuals all over this community in throat-swollen adoration to follow the commandment to pray one for another.*

At this moment, we collectively target Sister Annie for a blessing. Take away her apprehension Jesus: Hold her hand even as God holds her in His palm.

In this place where we have heard so much sad news of late, Death, injury, disappearance, and separation, let us hear some good news: that sister Annie's activities need not be restricted, that she is certifiably healthy as a horse. That she has many years to continue her mission of getting people within ear-shot of Brother John's altar call.

Father, we have asked for a blessing, a visible blessing, not as a sign, we know you exist. We just want a healthy, vibrant Annie and Lord while we are all teared up at being in your will; give us a healthy Martha, Gloria, Ramona, and guide Cindy at this time of trial in her life. Give her a happy marriage. AMEN

John did not realize how much these men loved him and Annie until that day. It was a humbling, heart-warming experience. As always, they had wonderful relationships that mitigated any pain they had. For example, John and a congregant both loved to fish and often John would go below Waterville dam's spillway and catch catfish like crazy.

As in John's other churches, numbers of people joined while John was there. He and Annie had good relationships with everyone. In fact, a local bridge group invited Annie to be a part of their group. Annie had never played bridge in her life, but a couple of the ladies took her under their wing and taught her how to play. As bridge players know, sometimes a bridge table has a dummy. One night, one of the ladies, Constance told Annie that she was the dummy. It broke Annie's heart. She did not know what the dummy was. She came home in tears and told John that they called her a dummy. John thought that the bridge sessions was the most fun Annie ever had.

In July of 2003, John had a light stroke. It left him in a condition that he could no longer do everything that the church deserved. He tried for several months but it was just too difficult. He talked with the deacons and told them that he was going to retire and apply for disability. They tried to get him to reconsider and just preach on

Sundays. John told them that might work for two or three months, but soon someone would complain about the preacher not doing his job. John retired and left the church at age sixty-two, exactly eight years after he had begun there. It was a difficult decision because both John and Annie genuinely loved this church family. In addition, Annie had a job that she liked better than any she previously had. She was the Executive Assistant to the President of First Capital Bank.

Not long before John retired, Mark and Hope had moved out of John and Annie's home. It gave them a chance to repaint and refinish the floors. Then, John, Annie, Mark, Luke, and a friend of Luke's loaded everything into trailers, pickups, and a U-Haul truck and headed back to Georgia. Without a doubt, the Lord saved the best for last for the Roberts. This was the most thoughtful, most cooperative church John had pastored since his very first church in [name state]Mississippi.

It felt good being home again, especially with Mark, Luke, and their families nearby. However, Annie went to work in another bank about as soon as they got back in the state. She was not able to get everything organized in the new house as soon as she had hoped. The first six months back, John could not do much of anything. He could not preach nor work in his woodshop. He just sat in the house surrounded by unpacked boxes. It was so discouraging, and a reoccurrence of chronic fatigue syndrome combined with the stroke was debilitating. But, as soon as he lost his energy, he began to regain it. Not long after that, a church about forty miles away asked if he would preach for them until they found a pastor. He accepted their invitation gladly. It felt wonderful to be back in the pulpit again and he stayed with them for about nine months until they called a pastor.

No sooner had he finished that interim position that a small country church asked if he would preach for them until they got a pastor. John is still preaching for them twelve years later. This church is not demanding on his time, so they are a perfect fit. John was able to get back in his shop and build furniture. After Annie retired at age sixty-two, they built furniture together. Their only advertising was by word of mouth. And, they sold a respectable number of custom pieces every year.

John's developed a chronic back problem during this time. Over the next few years, he would have four surgeries on his spine. This and arthritis, scoliosis, and a terrible degenerative disk disease limited what John could do, and he tried again to get the church to call a full-time pastor, but they would not hear of it. John was out of the pulpit months at a time.

As he serves this church as an interim pastor, he has helped the church to upgrade its buildings, which was a costly endeavor. One day the chairman of deacons said to John, "Let me run something by you. I think our church needs a new fellowship hall, what do you think?" John responded that he thought it was a great idea and long overdue. The deacons met and all agreed that they needed one. Thankfully, the church approved, and they selected a contractor. Within a few weeks, the church had a beautiful new fellowship hall with bathrooms. The church was able to build this much-needed addition without borrowing. It has been one of the best things the church has done.

Not long after that project, the church decided to fix the floor in the sanctuary because it was sagging toward the middle. Upon further examination, dry rot in this one-hundred and seventy-five-year-old church had done some irreparable damage to the entire floor structure. Contractors were contacted again, and they gave the entire building a thorough inspection. Their recommendation was to remove the entire roof system - in other words, take the entire top off the sanctuary and replace it with trusses, new metal roof, and new drop ceiling because of severe structural problems. They also suggested removing the entire floor system and replacing it with a new one. This would call for a new interior painting and new carpet in the sanctuary. They would have to move into the fellowship hall for two to three months.

The proposed renovations caused John untold stress because not everyone believed that they were necessary. Numerous deacons and committee meetings took place and sometimes tempers flared. John spent a lot of time trying to keep peace and getting as much advice from contractors as he could. This rocked on for more than a year and finally, the deacons all came to an agreement that they ought to go ahead for the future generation. The recommendation was presented to the church one Sunday morning. The following Sunday, the vote overwhelmingly passed the construction recommendation. The contractor and John decided to wait until the spring weather breaks before beginning. That gave the church time to digest all that was to be involved and get ready for the move to the fellowship hall. Again, this is something the church will be able to do despite the tens of thousands of dollars it will cost, without owing a penny when the job was finished.

John is still preaching at the church despite the severe back pain Some Sundays John can hardly get to the truck for the trip to the church. Standing in the pulpit to preach is tortuous many services. John is somewhat concerned because he has developed a new and different pain in his back. His surgeon has already told him unless something else went wrong he would carry this pain to heaven with him. Annie has been one of the best caregivers that God ever made She has made sure that John is taken care of better than if he were in a hospital. Truth be told, she has done not only her work but most of John's as well. Mark, Luke, and their wives have all been quite attentive to John and Annie's needs. John will stay on at the church as long as they need him or until he can no longer bear the pain. He still has concerns about his lymphoma. The oncologist says that eventually it will crop up somewhere else. For now, he is blessed for it to be in remission. John and Annie often talk about the seeming impossibility that these two Mississippi kids who were as green as gourds when they married could be as old as they are and have great-grandchildren.

It has been quite an experience from the time God called John met Annie to the present. John has conducted all too many funerals for the friends they made in the various churches they have served. Every funeral gets harder because of the time John and Annie were friends with the deceased and their families. John often wishes he had kept track of the numbers of weddings and funerals he conducted over the years. And John is thrilled that one more wedding is on the horizon. He has been asked to perform the wedding ceremony for his grandson, Timothy, and his fiancé, Ruth later this year. He cannot get his mind wrapped around the idea that this grandchild is getting married.

John and Annie still live in the house they built thirty-two years ago. They still enjoy building furniture in the workshop. Looking back over the years, John and Annie have been blessed a thousand times over by the experiences they enjoyed in the churches they served. Despite the lingering illness and pain. Despite the good times and the times not so good in the churches he served John would tell you that he still believes *the best is yet to be*. And the best is when we stand in the presence of Jesus and hear Him say about our sin, FORGIVEN!

Would it surprise you to learn that ministers are imperfect people? Well, gasp, they are. But, in this perfectly delightful narrative, Bryant captures - with humor and honesty - the nuisances and joys of his 55 years of experience as a Baptist minister living in the deep South.

From Navy serviceman to vacuum salesman to radio personality to cancer survivor, Bryant describes how he ultimately finds his way to the pastorate.

His sometimes irreverent (but always kind) descriptions of church members and his own foibles make this an entertaining and inspiring read for anyone – believers and non-believers alike.

Melinda Ruben

Greenseed Tutoring, Writing, and Editing

Boca Raton, Florida

Bryant has authored articles for Church Administration Magazine and GoodNews Christian Magazine as well as having this book available on Amazon Kindle.

Bryant, a native of Booneville, Mississippi lives in Summerville, Georgia with his wife of 58 years. They have two sons, three grandchildren and two great grandchildren.

He graduated from Northeast Mississippi Junior College in Booneville, Mississippi with an Associate of Arts degree. Graduated from Blue Mountain College in Blue Mountain, Mississippi with a Bachelor of Arts degree with a double major in Bible and Social Studies; He attended the University of North Alabama in Florence, Alabama where he did master's work in Psychology. He also took extensive training at the State Mental Hospital in Bolivar, Tennessee.

Bryant pastored seven churches in fifty-five years of ministry and currently serves a rural church in Summerville, Georgia as Interim Pastor.